HANUMAN

HANUMAN WAS THE CHILD OF PAVANA, THE WIND GOD. ONE DAY HE SAW THE RISING SUN AND THINKING IT TO BE AN APPLE, HE LEAPT TOWARDS IT.

AS HE GREW, HIS STRENGTH GREW WITH HIM. ONE DAY, WITH HIS BARE HANDS, HE SAVED PRINCE SUGREEVA, FROM THE CHARGE OF A WILD ELEPHANT.

THANKS FOR YOUR TIMELY HELP, HANUMAN!

PRINCE SUGREEVA, I'M HONOURED!

WHEN VALI, THE KING OF KISH-KINDHA BANISHED HIS BROTHER, SUGREEVA, FROM HIS KINGDOM, HANUMAN WENT WITH HIM TO THE JUNGLES NEAR THE RIVER PAMPA. THERE THEY LIVED A HARD LIFE.

ONE DAY—

THERE ARE TWO MEN COMING THIS WAY.

HAVE THEY COME FROM VALI? HANUMAN! PLEASE GO AND FIND OUT WHO THEY ARE.

HANUMAN ASSUMED THE FORM OF A POOR MAN AND APPRO-ACHED THE *STRANGERS*.

WHERE ARE YOU ASCETICS GOING, SIR?

WE ARE LOOKING FOR SUGREEVA, THE VANARA KING.

THIS IS MY ELDER BROTHER RAMA, THE BANISHED PRINCE OF AYODHYA. HIS WIFE SITA WAS ABDUCTED BY RAVANA, THE DEMON KING. WE WANT SUGREEVA TO HELP US FIND SITA.

LISTENING TO LAXMANA, HANU-MAN'S HEART WAS SUDDENLY FILLED WITH A STRANGE FEELING OF LOVE AND ADORATION.

HANUMAN THREW AWAY HIS DISGUISE AND FELL PROSTRATE AT RAMA'S FEET.

FORGIVE ME, I'M REALLY HANUMAN, SUGREEVA'S MINISTER.

WILL YOU TAKE US TO SUGREEVA?

HANUMAN JOYFULLY CARRIED RAMA AND LAXMANA ON HIS SHOULDERS.

IT WAS A HAPPY MEETING. THE TWO BROTHERS KNEW, THEY HAD FOUND FRIENDS.

WILL YOU HELP ME KILL VALI?

WHY DO YOU WANT TO KILL YOUR BROTHER?

"ONCE VALI AND I HAD GONE TO FIGHT A DEMON. THERE WAS A BIG CAVE. VALI ASKED ME TO WAIT OUTSIDE AND WENT IN. WHEN HE DID NOT COME OUT FOR A LONG TIME, I THOUGHT HE WAS DEAD AND CAME BACK.

"THE THRONE COULD NOT REMAIN VACANT. THE PEOPLE CROWNED ME AS KING. THEN ONE DAY VALI CAME BACK..."

"...AND DROVE ME AWAY."

SINCE THEN I HAVE BEEN RUNNING FROM HIM. WILL YOU HELP ME TO KILL HIM?

YES, I WILL!

SUGREEVA BROUGHT A SMALL BUNDLE TO RAMA.

WE SAW A LADY BEING CARRIED AWAY IN RAVANA'S CHARIOT. SHE THREW THESE DOWN TO US.

YES, THESE ARE SITA'S JEWELS.

SUGREEVA CALLED VALI TO A DUEL. RAMA WAITED FOR A CHANCE TO KILL VALI. BUT HE COULD NOT RECOGNISE HIM. BOTH THE BROTHERS LOOKED ALIKE.

FOR THE NEXT ROUND, RAMA GAVE SUGREEVA A GARLAND TO WEAR. THIS TIME HIS ARROW FOUND ITS MARK.

SUGREEVA WAS CROWNED THE KING OF KISH-KINDHA. VALI'S SON ANGADA BECAME THE CROWN PRINCE.

LONG LIVE KING SUGREEVA!

LONG LIVE PRINCE ANGADA!

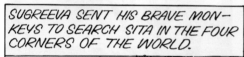

SUGREEVA SENT HIS BRAVE MON-KEYS TO SEARCH SITA IN THE FOUR CORNERS OF THE WORLD.

WE MUST LOOK EVERYWHERE!

WE MUST FIND HER!

THE MONKEYS WENT OUT IN DIFFERENT DIRECTIONS.

HANUMAN, ANGADA AND JAMBA-VAAN WENT SOUTH, UNTIL THEY CAME TO THE OCEAN.

ON A HILL NEARBY THEY MET THE VULTURE KING.

ACROSS THE OCEAN LIES LANKA - RAVANA'S CAPITAL CITY. SITA IS A PRI-SONER THERE.

A GIANT MOUNTAIN SUDDENLY ROSE FROM THE OCEAN AND BLOCKED HANUMAN'S WAY. HANUMAN STRUCK THE MOUNTAIN WITH HIS CHEST.

I AM MAINAKA. YOUR FATHER HAD ONCE SAVED MY LIFE. YOU MUST WAIT FOR A WHILE!

THANK YOU! BUT I CANNOT WAIT!

AS HANUMAN WENT FLYING, SURASA, THE SEA MONSTER CAME OUT WITH HER JAWS WIDE OPEN.

YOU MUST ENTER MY MOUTH!

HANUMAN STARTED BLOWING HIM-SELF UP BIGGER AND BIGGER...

...AND THE MONSTER OPENED HER JAWS WIDER AND WIDER.

SUDDENLY HANUMAN BECAME VERY SMALL AND BEFORE THE MONSTER COULD REALISE IT, HE ENTERED HER MOUTH AND CAME OUT AGAIN.

YOUR WISH IS FULFILLED. I DID ENTER YOUR MOUTH.

YOU ARE BRAVE. I WAS ONLY TESTING YOUR DETERMINATION.

AT LAST HANUMAN REACHED THE SHORES OF LANKA.

9

HOW SHALL I ENTER THE CITY? THERE ARE GUARDS ALL AROUND. LET ME BECOME SMALL. NOBODY WILL NOTICE ME.

HANUMAN ROAMED THE CITY FROM STREET TO STREET, FROM HOUSE TO HOUSE...

...THERE WERE MIGHTY WAR ELEPHANTS...

...DEADLY WEAPONS...

...AND GIANT WARRIORS GUARDING THE WALLS.

LANKA WAS A DAZZLING, BEAUTIFUL CITY. BUT HANUMAN WAS SOMEWHAT SAD.

ALL THIS WILL BE DESTROYED WHEN MY MASTER COMES TO FIGHT RAVANA.

AFTER SURVEYING THE CITY, HANUMAN WENT INTO RAVANA'S PALACE.

IT WAS NIGHT. THE WHOLE PALACE WAS ASLEEP...

...THERE WERE THE BEAUTIFUL QUEENS...

THERE WAS INDRAJIT-RAVANA'S WARRIOR SON.

AND KUMBHAKARNA, RAVANA'S BROTHER, WHO SLEPT SIX MONTHS OF THE YEAR.

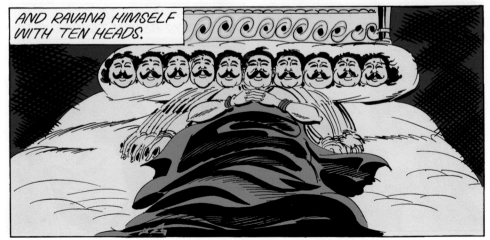

AND RAVANA HIMSELF WITH TEN HEADS.

IN RAVANA'S CHAMBER, HANUMAN SAW A BEAUTIFUL WOMAN ASLEEP.

IS SHE SITA? NO, NEVER! HOW COULD I THINK SHE WOULD GIVE HERSELF TO THIS BRUTE?

NOT FINDING SITA IN THE PALACE, HANUMAN WENT TO THE ASHOKA GARDEN ADJOINING THE PALACE.

UNDER A TREE SAT SITA, SLEEPLESS, THINKING OF RAMA.

I CAN'T APPROACH HER! SHE IS SURROUNDED BY DEMONS.

HANUMAN REMAINED HIDDEN IN A TREE. IN THE DAWN CAME RAVANA.

ARE YOU STILL DETERMINED NOT TO BE MY WIFE?

IT'S WRONG TO TALK LIKE THAT.

I CAN HEAR THE TWANG OF MY HUSBAND'S BOW. YOUR DAYS ARE NUMBERED.

HA! WHAT CAN RAMA DO?

AFTER RAVANA HAD GONE, THE RAKSHASIS BEGAN TEASING SITA.

MARRY HIM! WHERE ELSE CAN YOU GET SUCH A HUSBAND?

HOW MUCH MORE CAN I ENDURE?

WHEN SITA WAS LEFT ALONE FOR SOME TIME, HANUMAN TOOK OUT THE SIGNET RING RAMA HAD GIVEN HIM AND DROPPED IT ON HER LAP.

WHAT IS THIS? MY HUSBAND'S RING?

HANUMAN CLIMBED DOWN FROM THE TREE AND STOOD IN FRONT OF SITA. HE RELATED EVERYTHING TO HER.

MY MASTER WILL SOON COME TO SAVE YOU!

I CAN CARRY YOU ON MY BACK. PLEASE COME WITH ME.

NO! FOR HIS HONOUR HE MUST COME AND FIGHT RAVANA. HERE, TAKE THIS JEWEL TO HIM. HE WILL KNOW.

HANUMAN DECIDED TO TEACH RAVANA A LESSON.

HOW DO YOU LIKE THAT?

THAT GOES FOR YOU!

UPROOTING TREES, BEATING RAKSHASAS, HANUMAN CREATED HAVOC IN RAVANA'S PALACE.

HELP!

IS HE A DEMON?

RUN FOR YOUR LIVES!

THE PANIC-STRICKEN RAKSHASAS RUSHED TO RAVANA.

A MONSTER HAS ENTERED THE GARDEN, YOUR MAJESTY!

RAVANA SENT HIS SOLDIERS TO CAPTURE HANUMAN. BUT NO ONE COULD COME NEAR HIM.

THEN CAME INDRA-JIT, RAVANA'S WARRIOR SON.

INDRAJIT COULD NOT SUBDUE HANUMAN WHO HAD BY NOW ASSUMED HIS NORMAL SIZE. THEN HE USED HIS MIGHTIEST WEAPON, THE SNAKE ARROWS. HANUMAN LAY MOTIONLESS, TIED BY THE COILS.

THE RAKSHASAS BOUND HIM TIGHTLY.

I SHALL NOT FREE MYSELF! THIS IS THE ONLY WAY I CAN ENTER RAVANA'S COURT.

HANUMAN WAS CARRIED INTO THE DAZZLING THRONE ROOM.

CALL THE EXECUTIONER!

VIBHEESHANA, RAVANA'S RIGHTEOUS BROTHER INTERVENED.

YOU CANNOT KILL A MESSENGER!

THE RAKSHASAS TIED PIECES OF CLOTH AROUND HANUMAN'S TAIL AND POURED OIL. BUT THE TAIL GREW...

...LONGER

BRING MORE CLOTH!

MORE OIL!

...AND STILL LONGER.

THERE IS NO MORE OIL.

TELL THE KING!

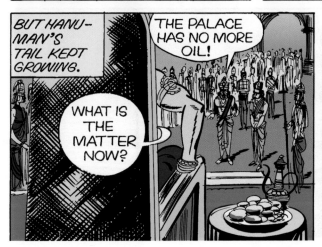

BUT HANU- MAN'S TAIL KEPT GROWING.

WHAT IS THE MATTER NOW?

THE PALACE HAS NO MORE OIL!

ALL RIGHT! LIGHT THE FLAME!

THE SOLDIERS TOOK HIM THROUGH THE STREETS.

FOOLS! THEY ARE SHOWING ME THE WHOLE PLAN OF THE CITY!

SUDDENLY HANUMAN SHRANK HIS SIZE. THE ROPES SLIPPED DOWN TO THE GROUND.

WITH A MIGHTY ROAR HE LEAPT TO A HOUSE TOP.

LONG LIVE RAMA! LONG LIVE SITA!

HANUMAN LEAPED FROM ONE HOUSETOP TO ANOTHER SETTING FIRE TO THE CITY.

HANUMAN WENT TO THE SEA TO EXTINGUISH HIS TAIL. HIS MISSION WAS MORE THAN COMPLETE.

ON THE OTHER SHORE, THE VANARAS PATIENTLY AWAITED HIS RETURN.

THERE HE COMES!

IN THEIR JOY, THE VANARAS LIFTED HANUMAN ABOVE THEIR HEADS AND DANCED AROUND.

LONG LIVE HANUMAN!

THE SEARCH PARTY AT LAST RETURNED HOME.

SITA'S CROWN JEWEL! MY DEAREST WIFE!

SUGREEVA ORDERED THE ARMY TO ASSEMBLE...

THE GREAT MONKEY ARMY FELL IN LINE...

...AND THE GIANT BEARS TOO!

17

THE GREAT ARMY REACHED THE SEASHORE. ON THE OTHER SIDE LAY LANKA WHERE SITA WAS A PRISONER.

HOW CAN WE CROSS THE MIGHTY OCEAN?

CAN'T WE BUILD A BRIDGE?

A BRIDGE? HOW?

NALA IS A GREAT ENGINEER MONKEY! HE CAN BUILD A BRIDGE!

MEANWHILE, VIBHEESHANA, RAVANA'S BROTHER HAD COME OVER TO JOIN RAMA.

I DO NOT WISH TO LIVE WITH MY SINFUL BROTHER WILL YOU GIVE ME SHELTER?

HOW CAN WE TRUST HIM?

THIS MAY BE A TRICK!

I THINK WE CAN BELIEVE HIM. HOWEVER, EVEN IF IT BE A TRICK, I CANNOT TURN AWAY SOMEONE WHO ASKS FOR SHELTER!

SOON NALA STARTED BUILDING A BRIDGE OF STONES.

THE HUGE STONES WERE RELAYED FROM HAND TO HAND DOWN THE MOUNTAINS...

...AND THE BRIDGE WAS READY.

THE ARMY STARTED OUT ON ITS MARCH.

TO LANKA!

TO LANKA!

HANUMAN CARRIED RAMA ON HIS SHOULDERS. ANGADA CARRIED LAXMANA.

THE OCEAN WAS CROSSED. RAMA'S ARMY REACHED LANKA. ON THE SEASHORE SURROUNDING THE CITY, THE ARMY SET UP CAMP.

SOME RAKSHASAS CAME TO RAMA'S CAMP DISGUISED AS MONKEYS.

HOW MANY MEN DO WE HAVE IN THE NORTH?

BUT VIBHEESHANA HAD SEEN THROUGH THEIR DISGUISE.

WHO IS LEADING THE SOUTH ATTACK?

HANU-MAN AND LAXMANA!

THESE ARE SPIES! SHALL WE KILL THEM?

NO, LET THEM GO. LET THEM TELL RAVANA WHAT HIS ENEMY IS LIKE!

PRINCE RAMA IS SO GENEROUS!

BEFORE THE BATTLE, RAVANA WENT TO A TOWER TO SURVEY THE ENEMY.

IN THE CENTRE THE CHARIOT BELONGS TO RAMA. INDRA GAVE IT TO HIM. TO HIS LEFT IS SUGREEVA!

HA! WE SHALL KILL THEM ALL!

THE BATTLE STARTED. THE MONKEYS ATTACKED WITH HUGE BOULDERS.

THE RAKSHASA GENERAL JAMBUMALI CAME TO FIGHT WITH HANUMAN. HANUMAN SMASHED HIS CHARIOT.

HANUMAN LIFTED RAMA AND LAXMANA TO HIS SHOULDERS. FROM THIS HIGH PERCH, THEIR ARROWS FOUND PERFECT MARKS.

DHUMRAKSHA CAME WITH A HUGE ARMY. HE WAS ONE OF RAVANA'S BEST GENERALS.

HANUMAN LIFTED HIM IN ONE HAND AND KILLED HIM.

NEXT TO COME WAS THE VICIOUS GIANT AKAMPANA. THE VANARAS RAN AWAY AT THE SIGHT OF HIM.

DON'T RUN AWAY! DON'T BE AFRAID!

HANUMAN UPROOTED A TREE AND KILLED AKAMPANA. HUNDREDS OF RAKSHASAS DIED CRUSHED BY THIS GIANT'S BODY.

WE MUST DESTROY THEM.

DO NOT WORRY, FATHER! I SHALL KILL THEM ALL! THEY CANNOT EVEN SEE ME.

AKAMPANA'S DEATH CAME AS A SHOCK TO RAVANA. MANY OF HIS GENERALS WERE DEAD. HIS GRIEF INCREASED HIS RAGE.

RAVANA'S SON INDRAJIT HAD RECEIVED A BOON FROM THE GODS. HE COULD FIGHT ANYONE WITHOUT BEING SEEN BY THE ENEMY.

LOOK! LAXMANA IS HIT BY AN ARROW!

WHEN THE BATTLE CEASED FOR THE DAY, (THEY NEVER FOUGHT AFTER SUNSET IN THOSE DAYS) ALL STOOD AROUND THE FALLEN LAXMANA, THEIR HEARTS HEAVY WITH GRIEF.

WHAT SHALL WE DO?

BRING THE PHYSICIAN.

HANUMAN RUSHED TO ANOTHER PART OF THE BATTLE FIELD WHERE HE FOUND SUSHENA.

WHERE ARE YOU TAKING ME?

YOU MUST CURE MY PRINCE!

I NEED SANJEEVANI PLANT TO CURE LAXMANA!

FAR AWAY ON THE GANDHAMADAN HILL STOOD THE SANJEEVANI TREE. ITS ROOT COULD BRING LAXMANA BACK TO LIFE. BRAVE HANUMAN STARTED ON ANOTHER LEAP.

HANUMAN COULD NOT LOCATE THE TREE FROM AMONGST HUNDRED OTHERS. BUT THERE WAS VERY LITTLE TIME.

WHICH IS THE SANJEEVANI TREE?

UNWILLING TO WASTE ANY MORE TIME, HANUMAN GREW IN SIZE AND LIFTED THE WHOLE MOUNTAIN IN HIS HANDS AND RETURNED TO LANKA.

LAXMANA WAS SOON CURED. NOT ONLY HE, BUT THOUSANDS OF OTHER MONKEYS CAME BACK TO LIFE.

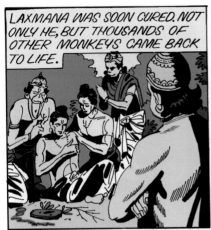

AS THE BATTLE STARTED AGAIN, RAVANA CAME OUT TO FIGHT IN HIS GOLDEN CHARIOT, HIS CROWN DAZZLING IN THE SUNLIGHT.

NO ONE COULD WITHHOLD HIS ATTACK. THEN RAMA, RIDING ON HANUMAN'S SHOULDERS, ATTACKED THE RAKSHA-SA KING.

RAMA'S ARROW CUT DOWN RAVANA'S CHARIOT. HE STOOD ON THE BATTLE GROUND, FACING DEATH.

YOU MAY GO NOW! I SHALL NOT KILL AN UNARMED ENEMY!

THE COUNCIL OF WAR IN RAVANA'S COURT.

WHO IS TO LEAD THE ARMY?

WAKE UP KU-MBHAKARNA!

KUMBHAKARNA USED TO SLEEP FOR SIX MONTHS AT A STRETCH.

PLEASE WAKE UP.

AT LAST, THE GIANT'S SLEEP WAS BROKEN.

WHAT IS THE MATTER?

YOU MUST GO TO BATTLE.

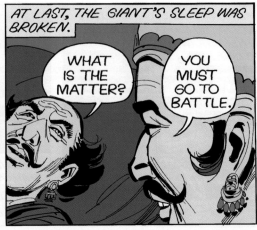

LIKE A TYPHOON, KUMBHAKARNA CAME TO THE BATTLE. THOUSANDS PERISHED UNDER HIS FEET.

RAMA'S ARROWS CUT HIS HEAD OFF.

RAVANA HAS NOBODY ELSE TO FIGHT FOR HIM.

INDRAJIT HAS GONE TO OFFER A SACRIFICE.

IF INDRAJIT COULD COMPLETE HIS SACRIFICIAL PRAYER, HE WOULD BECOME INVINCIBLE. BUT HIS PRAYER WAS NOT COMPLETED.

WHEN THE NEWS OF INDRA-JIT'S DEATH REACHED RAVANA—

I AM ALL ALONE NOW! BUT I'M STILL THE MIGHTIEST.

IT WAS TIME FOR THE LAST BATTLE. RAVANA CAME TO THE GATES OF LANKA. OUTSIDE, THE VANARA ARMY WAITED.

RAVANA RODE ON HIS CHARIOT, LIKE LIGHTNING, TEARING THROUGH THE RANKS OF THE VANARA ARMY.

RAVANA WAS A GREAT WARRIOR. THE BATTLE THAT RAGED WAS FIERCE.

AT LAST RAVANA CAME FACE TO FACE WITH RAMA. RAMA PICKED UP HIS BOW FOR THE LAST ARROW OF THIS GREAT BATTLE.

THE EVIL ENEMY HAD BEEN DESTROYED. VIRTUE HAD WON OVER GREED AND LUST.

THE KING HAD DIED. THE CITY OF LANKA WAS DARK AND MOURNFUL.

VIBHEESHANA WAS CROWNED THE KING OF LANKA.

SOON THE TRIUMPHAL MARCH BEGAN, OVER THE OCEAN, THE WAY THEY HAD COME.

COME MY BELOVED! YOU CAME IN THIS FLYING CHARIOT IN DISGRACE! YOU SHALL RETURN IN HONOUR!

AT LAST IT WAS TIME FOR RAMA'S RETURN TO AYODHYA. HANUMAN WENT AHEAD WITH THE NEWS.

I BRING HAPPY TIDINGS! FOURTEEN YEARS OF EXILE ARE OVER. THE MASTER IS COMING HOME.

THE WHOLE CITY ASSEMBLED TO WELCOME THE RETURNING PRINCES. THERE WAS JOY ALL AROUND.

LONG LIVE KING RAMA!

LONG LIVE PRINCE LAXMANA!

LONG LIVE QUEEN SITA!

THE TIME FOR PARTING HAD COME.

MY GOOD FRIENDS! YOU MUST GO BACK TO YOUR HOMES NOW!

CALL US ANY TIME YOU NEED OUR SERVICE!

BUT HANUMAN DID NOT GO.

WHAT ABOUT YOU, DEAR HANUMAN?

I SHALL STAY AND SERVE YOU FOR EVER.

The route to your roots

HANUMAN TO
THE RESCUE

Rama was frantic. His beloved brother lay dying and the only cure was tucked away on a forested mountainside far, far to the north. Big-hearted Hanuman could not bear to see their pain. He swelled into a giant; he flew; he battled deadly crocodiles and murderous ogres; he pitted his wits against powerful gods – all to deliver the precious medicinal plant, Sanjeevani, before it was too late. He brought the entire mountain to rest at Rama's feet!

Script
Luis M.Fernandes

Illustrations
Ram Waeerkar

Editor
Anant Pai

HANUMAN TO THE RESCUE

WHEN RAMA THE EXILED PRINCE OF AYODHYA ATTACKED LANKA, RAVANA, THE KING OF LANKA, HIMSELF RODE OUT ONE DAY TO THE BATTLEFIELD.

IN THE COURSE OF THE DAY'S BATTLE, HE HURLED HIS SPEAR AT RAMA'S BROTHER, LAKSHMANA.

EVEN AS LAKSHMANA FELL...

...RAMA CAME FORWARD...

...AND DROVE AWAY THE MIGHTY RAKSHASA.

LAKSHMANA! LAKSHMANA!

OH, MY NOBLE BROTHER... WHERE WILL I FIND ANOTHER LIKE YOU?

SAVE HIM, SUSHENA. YOU ARE A GREAT PHYSICIAN.

LIFE HAS NOT LEFT HIM AS YET. I COULD EASILY REVIVE HIM WITH THE HERB CALLED VISHALYA KARANI.

BUT I MUST GET IT BEFORE DAYBREAK.

WHERE IS THIS HERB TO BE FOUND?

ON MOUNT GANDHAMADANA.

BUT IT WOULD TAKE EIGHTEEN YEARS TO GO THERE AND COME BACK!

I COULD DO IT IN MUCH LESS THAN EIGHTEEN HOURS.

GO, HANUMAN. LOOK FOR A GOLDEN CREEPER WITH BLUE FLOWERS.

IT GROWS ON EITHER SIDE OF THE RIVER WHICH FLOWS DOWN ONE OF THE PEAKS OF MOUNT GANDHA-MADANA.

I SHALL LEAVE AT ONCE.

CAST ASIDE YOUR ANXIETIES, LORD RAMA. LAKSHMANA WILL BE SAVED.

THEN HANUMAN, THE SON OF THE WIND, MADE HIMSELF LARGER AND LARGER···

···AND WITH ONE GREAT LEAP···

···ROSE HIGH UP INTO THE SKY.

AS HE FLEW ALONG, SUPPORTED BY THE WIND, RAVANA SAW HIM FROM LANKA.

WHERE DOES HANUMAN GO AT THIS HOUR? AH! THE VISHALYA KARANI! THE ONLY HERB THAT CAN SAVE LAKSHMANA!

SEND KALANEMI TO ME!

KALANEMI WAS A FEARFUL MONSTER WITH FOUR HEADS, EIGHT EYES AND EIGHT ARMS. HE WAS ALSO A MAGICIAN.

DID YOU SEND FOR ME, RAVANA?

YES, UNCLE KALANEMI, I NEED YOUR HELP.

HANUMAN IS ON HIS WAY TO MOUNT GANDHAMADANA TO GET THE VISHALYA-KARANI FOR LAKSHMANA WHOM I WOUNDED IN BATTLE TODAY.

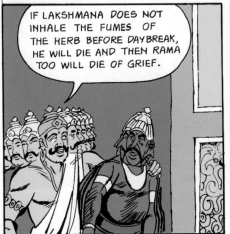

IF LAKSHMANA DOES NOT INHALE THE FUMES OF THE HERB BEFORE DAYBREAK, HE WILL DIE AND THEN RAMA TOO WILL DIE OF GRIEF.

GO TO MOUNT GANDHA-MADANA AND DESTROY HANUMAN WITH YOUR MAGIC.

DESTROY HANUMAN?

I'LL GIVE YOU HALF MY KINGDOM, IF YOU SUCCEED.

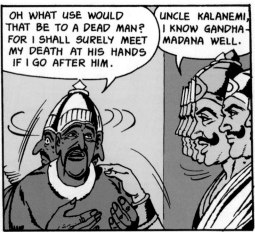

OH WHAT USE WOULD THAT BE TO A DEAD MAN? FOR I SHALL SURELY MEET MY DEATH AT HIS HANDS IF I GO AFTER HIM.

UNCLE KALANEMI, I KNOW GANDHA-MADANA WELL.

THERE'S A FEROCIOUS CROCODILE PROWLING IN THE RIVER THERE. ALL YOU HAVE TO DO IS...

NO, RAVANA! I CANNOT GO TO GANDHAMADANA. THE SON OF THE WIND IS CUNNING. HE'LL DASH OUT MY BRAINS, THE MOMENT HE DISCOVERS WHO I AM. YOU KNOW HOW...

GO AT ONCE!

Y-YES.

WHAT A PREDICAMENT. I AM DEAD IF I GO AND DEAD IF I DON'T.

KALANEMI USED HIS MAGIC...

...TO TRANSPORT HIMSELF TO MOUNT GANDHAMADANA.

THERE HE TRANSFORMED HIMSELF INTO A HERMIT...

...CREATED A BEAUTIFUL HERMITAGE OUT OF THIN AIR...

...AND SAT DOWN OUTSIDE IT.

HE SHOULD BE COMING ALONG ANY MOMENT NOW.

AH...THERE HE IS!

GREETINGS, HOLY SIR.

A GUEST!

WHAT GREAT GOOD FORTUNE IT IS TO HAVE A GUEST!

GO AND BATHE IN THAT RIVER, MY CHILD AND THEN YOU CAN REFRESH YOURSELF ON FRUITS.

I AM IN GREAT HASTE, SIR.

I HAVE NO TIME FOR FOOD AND DRINK. I AM LOOKING FOR A HERB CALLED VISHALYA-KARANI.

YOUR QUEST CAN WAIT.

HOW CAN I SEND YOU AWAY WITH-OUT FEEDING YOU? IF ONE FAILS TO PERSUADE HIS GUEST TO EAT, HE IS SURE TO BE DOOMED.

8

IT MOVED FORWARD SILENTLY AND SWIFTLY.

BUT HANUMAN SAW IT APPROACHING.

HE LUNGED FORWARD...

...CAUGHT HOLD OF THE REPTILE...

...AND FLUNG IT TO THE SHORE.

THEN HE POUNCED ON IT AND TORE OPEN ITS BREAST.

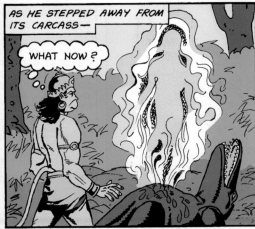

AS HE STEPPED AWAY FROM ITS CARCASS—

WHAT NOW?

I AM A CELESTIAL DANCER.

ONCE WHEN I WAS DANCING, MY FOOT ACCIDENTALLY TOUCHED THE PERSON OF INDRA.

HE WAS SO ENRAGED THAT HE TURNED ME INTO A CROCODILE... AND DECREED THAT I SHOULD LIVE IN THIS RIVER TILL I WAS LIBERATED BY YOU.

BEWARE OF THE FALSE HERMIT, O SON OF THE WIND !

THE FALSE HERMIT ?

KALANEMI MEANWHILE WAS MAKING PLANS FOR THE FUTURE.

I MUST MAKE SURE I GET THE BEST HALF OF LANKA. THE WESTERN COAST COULD GET FLOODED. I'LL TAKE THE EASTERN PART.

AS FOR THE WEALTH IN THE TREASURE HOUSES EVERYTHING WILL BE DIVIDED EQUALLY. SO TOO THE HORSES AND THE ELEPHANTS.

AND I'LL TAKE THE BEAUTIFUL QUEEN MANDO-DARI FOR MYSELF.

...COILING HIS TAIL ROUND HIM...

...HURLED HIM INTO THE SKY.

THE RAKSHASA SHOT THROUGH THE HEAVENS LIKE A COMET...

...AND LANDED...

...IN LANKA, AT RAVANA'S COURT.

IT'S KALANEMI! HE HAS FAILED IN HIS MISSION. THAT HERB MUST NOT REACH LAKSHMANA!

SUMMON THE SUN. QUICKLY!

RAVANA WAS THE MASTER OF THE THREE WORLDS AND THE SUN, TOO, HAD TO OBEY HIM. WHEN HE CAME —

LISTEN TO ME. YESTERDAY, I GRIEVOUSLY WOUNDED LAKSHMANA...

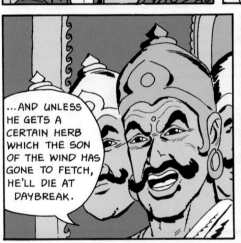

...AND UNLESS HE GETS A CERTAIN HERB WHICH THE SON OF THE WIND HAS GONE TO FETCH, HE'LL DIE AT DAYBREAK.

I WANT YOU TO HASTEN THAT HOUR.

GO AND RISE FROM YOUR APPOINTED PLACE.

NOW?

YES, NOW!

BUT, LORD OF LANKA...

GO!

SOME TIME LATER, HANUMAN WHO WAS SEARCHING FRANTICALLY FOR THE HERB, WAS STARTLED TO SEE A ROSY GLOW ON THE HORIZON.

WHAT! IS THE SUN READY TO RISE?

I MUST STOP HIM AT ONCE!

THE SUN GOD'S CHARIOTEER WAS STARTLED TO SEE A HUGE MONKEY DROPPING DOWN FROM THE SKY AND BARRING THE ROAD TO THE EAST.

HE WHIPPED HIS HORSES ROUND TOWARDS THE WEST.

BUT HANUMAN WAS TOO QUICK FOR HIM. HE DARTED FORWARD...

... CAUGHT HOLD OF THE CHARIOT...

...AND BEGAN TO WHIRL IT ROUND AND ROUND.

STOP! STOP!

WHAT'S GOING ON?

A HUGE MONKEY HAS TURNED OVER THE CHARIOT!

I SHALL BURN HIM AND FLING HIM DOWN TO EARTH.

OH-OH! I'D BETTER BE CAREFUL.

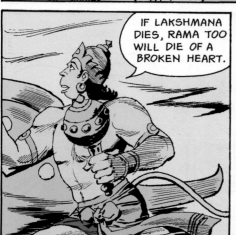

AS THE SUN LEANED FORWARD ...

...HANUMAN CAUGHT HIM IN A WARM EMBRACE.

AND BEFORE HE KNEW WHAT WAS HAPPENING BUNDLED HIM UNDER HIS ARM.

THEN HE RUSHED BACK TO GANDHAMADANA.

NOT MUCH TIME LEFT. SUSHENA SAID IT'S A GOLDEN CREEPER WITH BLUE FLOWERS...

...BUT I CAN'T SEE ANY SUCH PLANT HERE.

AS HE WAS WANDERING AROUND, HE CAME ACROSS SOME GANDHARVAS. THEY WERE SINGING AND DANCING.

THEY WILL KNOW WHERE I CAN FIND THE HERB.

GOOD PEOPLE, PLEASE TELL ME WHERE I COULD FIND THE PLANT CALLED VISHALYA-KARANI...

THERE HAS BEEN A GREAT BATTLE BETWEEN MY MASTER, RAMA AND THE LORD OF LANKA. RAMA'S BROTHER LAKSHMANA LIES AT DEATH'S DOOR.

WHAT IS HE TALKING ABOUT?

AND WHAT IS THAT GLOW AROUND HIS ARMPIT?

WE HAVE NEVER HEARD OF ANYONE CALLED RAMA. THE ONLY KINGS WE KNOW ARE OUR OWN—THE GREAT HOO HOO AND HA HA.

NOW TELL US WHY YOU HAVE REALLY COME HERE.

LET GO OF ME.

THE GANDHARVAS CROWDED ROUND HIM, TEASING HIM AND PULLING AT HIS HAIR. HANUMAN WAS ENRAGED.

HE MADE HIMSELF AS HUGE AS A HILL...

...AND STRUCK BACK AT HIS TORMENTORS.

YIEEEE!

HELP!

PRESENTLY, THE KINGS OF THE LAND, HOO HOO AND HA HA CAME TO BATTLE WITH HIM.

BUT HANUMAN PULLED THEIR BOWS AWAY FROM THEM...

...AND BROKE THEM.

PANDEMONIUM BROKE OUT AMONG THE GANDHARVAS AND HANUMAN WOULD HAVE DESTROYED THEM ALL IF HE HAD NOT SUDDENLY REMEMBERED HIS REASON FOR BEING THERE.

I CAN'T WASTE TIME FIGHTING THESE PEOPLE.

RAMA AND THE OTHERS MUST BE WAITING ANXIOUSLY FOR MY RETURN.

NOW I MUST RUSH TO LANKA.

RAMA AND EVERYONE ELSE WERE AMAZED TO SEE HANUMAN DESCENDING WITH A HUGE MOUNTAIN.

LATER, WHEN HE HAD LOWERED HIS LOAD, AND EXPLAINED HIS DIFFICULTY IN FINDING THE HERB, SUSHENA HIMSELF WENT UP WITH HIM AND GATHERED THE PLANTS HE WANTED.

THEN THE PHYSICIAN WENT BACK TO THE CAMP, MADE A PASTE OUT OF THE HERBS...

...AND HELD IT TO LAKSHMANA'S NOSE.

AS THE FUMES ENTERED HIS NOSTRILS —

HE IS STIRRING!

AFTER A WHILE —

RAMA!

LAKSHMANA!

LAKSHMANA IS SAFE.

VICTORY TO RAMA.

LATER —

I AM INDEBTED TO YOU, O SON OF THE WIND. NOW PLEASE TAKE THE MOUNTAIN BACK.

I'LL DO THAT AT ONCE.

SO ONCE AGAIN, HANUMAN PICKED UP MOUNT GANDHAMADANA...

...AND SET OFF ACROSS THE SKY.

AS HE WAS PASSING OVER RAVANA'S CAPITAL —

HANUMAN WILL NOT ESCAPE ME THIS TIME.

BUT AS THEY MOVED CLOSER, HE SUDDENLY SHOT OUT HIS TAIL...

...AND BEFORE THEY KNEW WHAT WAS HAPPENING, COILED IT ROUND SIX OF THEM.

THEN RAISING HIS TAIL HIGH UP...

...HE FLUNG THEM DOWN.

THE SURVIVING RAKSHASA FLED IN TERROR.

HE PROVED TOO STRONG FOR US, O LORD OF LANKA. I ESCAPED, BUT THE OTHERS ARE DEAD.

THIS IS INCREDIBLE!

HE IS MORE FORMIDABLE THAN I THOUGHT.

HANUMAN CONTINUED ON HIS WAY AND...

...RESTORED THE MOUNTAIN TO ITS ORIGINAL PLACE.

BEFORE I GO, I MUST HEAL THE GANDHARVAS I WOUNDED DURING OUR BATTLE.

HE CRUSHED SOME LEAVES OF THE PLANT WHICH HAD HEALED LAKSHMANA...

...DROPPED THEM INTO WATER...

...AND SPRINKLED THE WATER OVER THE GANDHARVAS.

ONE BY ONE THE GANDHARVAS BEGAN TO SIT UP.

WHAT HAPPENED?

WHERE AM I?

LOOK, THERE'S THE MONKEY WHO ATTACKED US!

BEAT HIM!

THE GANDHARVAS RUSHED AT HANUMAN.

HANUMAN DID NOT WAIT TO FIGHT THEM.

HE LEAPT UP...

28

...AND SPED BACK TO LANKA.

HIS COMRADES RAISED A LOUD CHEER WHEN THEY SAW HIM.

HANUMAN HAS RETURNED!

AS HANUMAN SALUTED RAMA—

WHAT IS THAT SHINING UNDER YOUR ARM, SON OF THE WIND?

OH, THAT IS THE SUN. RAVANA HAD ORDERED HIM TO RISE BEFORE THE APPOINTED HOUR.

SO I HAD TO HOLD HIM PRISONER.

HOW EXTRAORDINARY! LET HIM GO AT ONCE.

HANUMAN LIFTED HIS ARM AND LET THE SUN GO.

THEN THEY ALL PAID HOMAGE TO THE SUN GOD AND HE DEPARTED...

...TO RISE FROM HIS USUAL PLACE.

YOU HAVE SAVED LAKSHMANA'S LIFE, HANUMAN.

I AM EVER INDEBTED TO YOU.

VICTORY TO HANUMAN!

The route to your roots

BHEEMA AND HANUMAN

Both are known for their extraordinary strength and valour. Both are the sons of Vayu, the wind god. Hanuman lived in the Tretayug serving Sri Rama while Bheema, a contemporary of Krishna, lived in the Dwaparyug. The Mahabharata narrates the story of an encounter between the two mighty brothers.

Script	Illustrations	Editor
Kamala Chandrakant	M.N.Nangare	Anant Pai

Cover illustration by: C.M.Vitankar

BHEEMA AND HANUMAN

WHEN THE FIVE PANDAVA BROTHERS WERE DECEITFULLY DEPRIVED OF THEIR KINGDOM BY THEIR JEALOUS COUSINS, THE KAURAVAS, THEY HAD TO GO INTO EXILE FOR THIRTEEN YEARS ALONG WITH THEIR WIFE, DRAUPADI. DHOUMYA, THEIR PRECEPTOR, ACCOMPANIED THEM.

WHILE THEY WERE IN THE FOREST, ARJUNA, THE THIRD PANDAVA, LEFT FOR INDRAKEELA TO ACQUIRE CELESTIAL WEAPONS FROM THE DEVAS.

NEARLY FIVE YEARS WENT BY, BUT ARJUNA DID NOT RETURN.

EVERYTHING IN THIS FOREST REMINDS ME OF HIM. I CAN'T BEAR THIS SEPARATION MUCH LONGER.

I, TOO, FEEL THE SAME. WITHOUT ARJUNA THIS FOREST SEEMS EMPTY.

WHY DON'T WE GO TO SOME OTHER FOREST?

I HAVE BEEN THINKING ABOUT IT, TOO. LET US SEE WHAT SAGE DHOUMYA HAS TO SAY.

AS YUDHISHTHIRA AND THE OTHERS WERE TALKING WITH SAGE DHOUMYA —

AH! HERE COMES SAGE LOMASHA.

SAGE LOMASHA HAD COME WITH GOOD NEWS.

ARJUNA'S MISSION HAS BEEN SUCCESSFUL! BUT THE DEVAS NEED HIM FOR A LITTLE WHILE LONGER.

IN THE MEAN TIME, HE HAS ASKED ME TO TAKE YOU TO ALL THE IMPORTANT HOLY PLACES, TO THE TOP OF THE GANDHAMADANA MOUNTAIN AND, FINALLY, TO KUBERA'S GARDENS.

HE WILL JOIN US THERE ON HIS RETURN.

SO THE PANDAVAS AND DRAUPADI SET OUT WITH THE SAGES. THE THOUGHT THAT THEY WOULD SOON BE WITH ARJUNA MADE THE JOURNEY EASIER.

LOOK! THE MOUNTAIN!

ISN'T IT BEAUTIFUL— THE GANDHAMADANA MOUNTAIN, ABODE OF THE DEMIGODS?

SOON THEY WERE CLIMBING THE MOUNTAIN.

BE VERY CAREFUL. THE PATH AHEAD IS NARROW AND STEEP.

WHEN THEY WERE NEARLY AT THE TOP —

BHEEMA, AS YOU ARE THE STRONGEST, DRAUPADI SHALL BE UNDER YOUR SPECIAL CARE.

IT WAS AS IF YUDHISHTHIRA HAD SENSED WHAT WAS COMING: THE NEXT MOMENT A VIOLENT DUST-STORM BROKE OUT.

ARE THE HEAVENS COMING DOWN?

O BHEEMA, HELP ME!

TAKING DRAUPADI BY THE HAND, BHEEMA PULLED HER UNDER A TREE.

THE WIND ABATED BUT IT WAS FOLLOWED BY HEAVY RAIN.

SUDDENLY, THE SKY CLEARED AND THE SUN CAME OUT.

YUDHISHTHIRA'S FIRST CONCERN WAS FOR DRAUPADI.

ARE YOU SAFE? CAN YOU WALK?

I AM QUITE ALL RIGHT — AND READY TO CARRY ON.

BUT A FEW MOMENTS AFTER THEY HAD STARTED —

BH - EE - MA! HE - ELP ME!

NAKULA, WHO WAS BEHIND HER, RAN FORWARD.

DRAUPADI!

O DRAUPADI!

WHEN HER FATHER ENTRUSTED HER TO US, HE THOUGHT SHE WOULD KNOW ONLY HAPPINESS. INSTEAD, HARDSHIP AND SORROW HAVE BEEN HER LOT!

DRAUPADI HAS FAINTED!

THE SAGES, TOO, HURRIED TOWARDS DRAUPADI...

... AND TRIED TO REVIVE HER.

DRAUPADI SLOWLY OPENED HER EYES.

THEY PLACED HER GENTLY ON A DEERSKIN AND MADE HER REST AGAINST A TREE.

YUDHISHTHIRA WAS WORRIED.

O BHEEMA, IT WILL BE HARD FOR DRAUPADI TO CROSS THE SNOW-BOUND PEAKS STILL AHEAD OF US.

WHY DON'T YOU AND SAHADEVA STAY HERE WITH HER? THE REST OF US WILL PROCEED AND RETURN LATER WITH ARJUNA.

BUT BHEEMA WOULD NOT HEAR OF IT.

I CAN'T LET YOU GO. LET'S HAVE NO MORE SEPARATIONS. YOU KNOW HOW WE SUFFERED WITHOUT ARJUNA.

AS YUDHISHTHIRA WONDERED WHAT TO DO, BHEEMA'S FACE SUDDENLY LIT UP.

GHATOTKACHA* GHATOTKACHA WILL CARRY HER. I HAVE ONLY TO THINK OF HIM AND HE WILL BE HERE.

THEN SUMMON HIM.

BHEEMA CLOSED HIS EYES, HIS THOUGHTS FIXED ON GHATOT-KACHA AND...

...IN A FARAWAY FOREST GHATOTKACHA SUDDENLY STOOD STILL.

MY FATHER NEEDS ME. COME WITH ME.

THE NEXT MOMENT—

FATHER, HERE I AM. COMMAND ME!

* SON OF BHEEMA AND HIDIMBA, A DEMONESS

GHATOTKACHA, YOU CAN FLY ANY- WHERE AT WILL. CARRY DRAUPADI AND FOLLOW US TO THE MOUNTAIN TOP.

FLY LOW, SO SHE DOES NOT BECOME UNEASY.

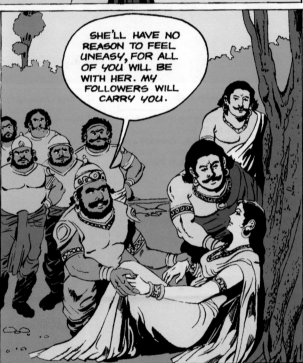

SHE'LL HAVE NO REASON TO FEEL UNEASY, FOR ALL OF YOU WILL BE WITH HER. MY FOLLOWERS WILL CARRY YOU.

CARRIED SWIFTLY BY THE RAKSHASAS . . .

9

···THEY ALIGHTED ON TOP OF THE MOUNTAIN.

AS THEY WALKED FARTHER—

THIS IS THE HOLY PLACE WHERE ONCE THE CELESTIAL SAGES, NARA AND NARAYANA, PERFORMED SEVERE PENANCE.

THE INHABITANTS OF THE PLACE RECEIVED THE PANDAVAS WITH HONOUR.

WELCOME TO OUR HERMITAGE, VIRTUOUS ONES!

LATER —

LET US REST HERE FOR A FEW DAYS.

SOME DAYS LATER, BHEEMA AND DRAUPADI WERE WALKING IN THE CHARMING WOODS OF THE HERMITAGE WHEN—

BHEEMA, LOOK AT THIS EXQUISITE FLOWER!

WHAT A SWEET FRAGRANCE IT HAS!

I'LL GIVE THIS ONE TO YUDHISH-THIRA. BUT I WOULD LIKE TO HAVE SOME MORE TO TAKE BACK WITH US.

OH, BHEEMA, GET THEM FOR ME!

THEN DRAUPADI RETURNED TO THE HERMITAGE

DEAR DRAUPADI, WE HAVE NOT BEEN ABLE TO GIVE YOU ALL THAT YOU DESERVE. I WOULD GO TO THE VERY ENDS OF THIS EARTH, IF NECESSARY, TO GET THE FLOWERS FOR YOU.

BHEEMA WENT IN THE DIRECTION FROM WHICH THE FLOWER HAD BLOWN TOWARDS THEM.

HE SEARCHED IN VAIN ALL OVER THE MOUNTAIN.

I HAVE LEFT THE OTHERS FOR TOO LONG. I MUST RETURN TO THE HERMITAGE.

BUT HOW CAN I RETURN WITHOUT THE FLOWERS?

I WILL TRY FOR A LITTLE WHILE LONGER.

HE WENT DEEPER AND DEEPER INTO THE FOREST.

SUDDENLY —

A ROGUE ELEPHANT !

SECONDS LATER, THE ELEPHANT WOULD HAVE CRUSHED HIM...

...BUT BHEEMA SEIZED IT BY THE TUSKS...

...AND DASHED IT TO THE GROUND.

POOR CREATURE! YOU LEFT ME NO CHOICE. I HAD TO KILL YOU!

HE WALKED ON, TERRIFYING THE ANIMALS WHICH CROSSED HIS PATH.

THEN HE CAME TO A CLEARING FROM WHERE HE COULD SEE A BANANA GROVE AT THE FOOT OF A MOUNTAIN.

HE STRODE TOWARDS IT DESTROYING EVERYTHING IN HIS PATH.

PERHAPS I'LL FIND THE FLOWERS ON THAT MOUNTAIN.

14

AS HE NEARED THE BANANA GROVE, HE SAW A LAKE.

HOW COOL AND REFRESHING IT LOOKS! I'LL TAKE A DIP BEFORE I ENTER THE GROVE.

A LITTLE LATER, BHEEMA CAME OUT OF THE WATER AND, RAISING HIS CONCH TO HIS LIPS, BLEW IT WITH ALL HIS MIGHT.

NOW I SHALL ENTER THAT GROVE.

UNKNOWN TO BHEEMA, THE GROVE WAS THE HOME OF HANUMAN.

ONLY ONE BEING ON EARTH CAN SOUND A CONCH SO LOUDLY — BHEEMA !

FROM THE GROVE HANUMAN SPIED BHEEMA AND BY HIS SPIRITUAL POWERS DIVINED HIS PURPOSE.

IT IS BHEEMA ! MY DEAR BROTHER ! HE HAS COME FOR THE CELESTIAL FLOWERS !

HANUMAN STRETCHED HIMSELF ACROSS THE NARROW PATH AT THE GROVE'S ENTRANCE.

BHEEMA WILL NEED MY GUIDANCE AND PROTECTION TO SUCCEED IN HIS QUEST.

TO ATTRACT BHEEMA'S ATTENTION HE BEGAN TO LASH HIS LONG TAIL ON THE GROUND AND TO ROAR.

BHEEMA HAS ALWAYS BEEN TOO PROUD OF HIS STRENGTH. FOR HIS OWN GOOD, I MUST TEACH HIM TO BE HUMBLE.

SO LOUD WERE THE SOUNDS HANUMAN MADE THAT THE MOUNTAIN SHOOK AND RUMBLED.

EVEN BHEEMA, FOR A MOMENT, KNEW FEAR!

THE DEAFENING SOUNDS COME FROM THE GROVE!

BUT HE STRODE UP TO THE GROVE. THE SIGHT HE SAW MADE HIM LAUGH WITH RELIEF.

HA! HA! HO! HO! IT'S ONLY A MONKEY! I'LL HAVE SOME FUN.

GOING CLOSER, HE GAVE A SUDDEN ROAR.

GR-R-R-R!

HANUMAN SIMPLY TURNED AND LOOKED LAZILY AT BHEEMA.

I AM ILL. I WAS ASLEEP AND YOU WOKE ME UP. BEING A MAN, YOU ARE WISER THAN I. YOU OUGHT TO BE MORE CONSIDERATE. WHO ARE YOU?

I AM BHEEMA, THE SON OF PANDU, BORN TO KUNTI THROUGH THE GRACE OF VAYU!

WHY HAVE YOU COME HERE? MERE MORTALS MAY NOT GO ANY FURTHER ALONG THIS PATH. BE SENSIBLE, AND GO BACK.

HOW DARE THIS MONKEY TALK TO ME LIKE THAT!

19

USING ALL HIS STRENGTH, HE TRIED AGAIN.

WHAT'S THE MATTER WITH ME? I, BHEEMA, AM UNABLE TO MOVE ASIDE THE TAIL OF A MERE MONKEY!

BUT IS IT A MERE MONKEY? NO, IT ISN'T! THEN WHO COULD IT BE?

O MIGHTY ONE, FORGIVE MY HARSH WORDS. PRAY TELL ME WHO YOU ARE.

I AM YOUR BROTHER, HANUMAN! BEYOND THIS PATH LIES HEAVEN....

BHEEMA FELL PROSTRATE BEFORE HANUMAN.

MY BROTHER! HANUMAN! I HAVE SEEN YOU! NO ONE IS MORE FORTUNATE THAN I AM. SHOW ME THE FORM IN WHICH YOU CROSSED THE OCEAN! PLEASE!

SUDDENLY, HANUMAN'S BODY GREW BIGGER AND BIGGER...

.... TILL IT ROSE HIGHER THAN THE GANDHAMADANA MOUNTAIN.

RETURNING TO HIS EARLIER SIZE, HANUMAN EMBRACED BHEEMA.

I FEEL A STRANGE POWER ENTER MY BODY!

MY FATIGUE HAS GONE! FILLED WITH YOUR STRENGTH AND YOUR BLESSINGS, O HANUMAN, WE ARE SURE TO CONQUER OUR ENEMIES.

I'LL DO MORE. WHEN YOU CHARGE AT THE ENEMY, I SHALL SIT ON ARJUNA'S FLAGSTAFF AND MY ROAR SHALL STRIKE TERROR INTO YOUR ENEMIES' HEARTS.

ENOUGH! I FEEL WEAK AND FAINT. THE LIGHT EMANATING FROM YOUR BODY DAZZLES ME!

HANUMAN THEN POINTED TO A PATH.

THAT PATH WILL TAKE YOU TO THE SAUGANDHIKA FOREST AND KUBERA'S FAVOURITE GARDENS. THERE YOU WILL FIND THE FLOWERS YOU ARE LOOKING FOR.

AT THE MOMENT OF PARTING, THE TIDE OF EMOTION THAT HE HAD STEMMED FOR SO LONG BROKE LOOSE. TEARS FLOWED DOWN HANUMAN'S FACE.

O, BHEEMA, MY EYES ARE BLESSED BY SEEING YOU. WHEN YOU GO BACK, YOU MAY SPEAK OF ME, BUT DON'T TELL ANYONE THAT I LIVE HERE.

AND HANUMAN VANISHED.

I MUST GET THE FLOWERS AND HURRY BACK TO THE HERMITAGE. YUDHISHTHIRA WILL BE ANXIOUS.

BHEEMA SPED ON . . .

. . . TILL HE REACHED THE LAKE IN THE SAUGANDHIKA FOREST WHERE THE LOTUS GREW.

AS BHEEMA BENT TO DRINK FROM THE LAKE —

WAIT! THIS IS KUBERA'S* FAVOURITE PLAYGROUND. MORTALS ARE NOT PERMITTED TO COME HERE.

WHO ARE YOU?

WHY HAVE YOU COME HERE?

* THE LORD OF THE DEMIGODS

25

WHEN BHEEMA EXPLAINED WHY HE HAD COME THERE —

YOU CANNOT DRINK THE WATER OF THIS LAKE OR CARRY AWAY THE FLOWERS WITHOUT KUBERA'S PERMISSION.

WHAT NONSENSE! THIS LAKE WHICH HAS SPRUNG UP ON THE MOUNTAIN BELONGS TO ALL.

YOU PROPOSE TO TAKE THE FLOWERS AWAY BY FORCE!

AND YOU SAY YOU ARE THE BROTHER OF YUDHISHTHIRA, THE RIGHTEOUS!

WITHOUT WAITING TO SAY ANY MORE, BHEEMA PLUNGED INTO THE LAKE FOLLOWED BY THE ANGRY RAKSHASAS.

BIND HIM!

SEIZE HIM!

CUT HIM DOWN!

EAT HIM UP!

BHEEMA TURNED UPON THEM IN A FURY.

AA-AH!

AH! MY ARM!

SAVE ME!

HE KILLED OVER A HUNDRED RAKSHASAS.

FLEE!

FLEE!

THE OTHER RAKSHASAS FLED THROUGH THE SKY . . .

. . . TILL THEY REACHED THE ABODE OF KUBERA.

LORD! YUDHISHTHIRA'S BROTHER HAS ENTERED THE LAKE WITHOUT YOUR PERMISSION.

WE TRIED TO STOP HIM BUT HE FOUGHT WITH US.

FORGIVE US.

TO THEIR ASTONISHMENT, KUBERA SMILED.

I KNOW WHY BHEEMA IS HERE! RETURN TO YOUR POSTS. LET HIM TAKE THE FLOWERS.

MEANWHILE, BHEEMA GATHERED THE RARE CELESTIAL FLOWERS.

THEN HE BEGAN TO FROLIC IN THE LAKE, THINKING OF DRAUPADI'S JOY AT RECEIVING THE FLOWERS.

SUCH WAS THE ZEST WITH WHICH HE MADE SPORT IN THE WATER THAT A VIOLENT STORM AROSE, WHICH WHIRLED WATER AND STONES AROUND.

FIERY METEORS BEGAN TO FALL. DREADFUL SOUNDS OF EXPLOSIONS RANG THROUGH THE SKY. THE EARTH BEGAN TO TREMBLE AND DUST FELL IN SHOWERS. BIRDS AND BEASTS CRIED IN SHRILL VOICES.

AT THE HERMITAGE, YUDHISHTHIRA WAS ALARMED.

O BROTHERS, ARM YOURSELVES. WE MAY SOON HAVE TO SHOW OUR MIGHT.

BUT WHERE IS BHEEMA?

ONLY THEN DID YUDHISHTHIRA REALISE THAT DRAUPADI WAS SMILING SERENELY.

DRAUPADI, IS BHEEMA BENT ON PERFORMING SOME GREAT ACT? OR HAS THAT HERO ALREADY ACHIEVED SOME GREAT FEAT?

O KING, HE MUST HAVE FOUND THE CELESTIAL LOTUSES.

DO YOU REMEMBER THE ONE I GAVE YOU? I HAD TOLD HIM TO BRING SOME MORE OF THEM FOR ME.

YUDHISHTHIRA TURNED IN ALARM TO GHATOTKACHA.

YOU KNOW WHERE THE LAKE IS. TAKE US THERE BEFORE HE OFFENDS THE CELESTIALS AND INCURS THEIR WRATH.

CARRIED BY GHATOTKACHA AND HIS RAKSHASAS, THEY SOON CAME TO THE LAKE.

AH! THERE HE IS! AND HE IS LOOKING VERY PLEASED!

30

O BHEEMA, WHAT HAVE YOU DONE ? IF YOU CARE FOR ME, YOU MUST NEVER AGAIN COMMIT SUCH RASH ACT !

BHEEMA MERELY SMILED IN REPLY AND GAVE THE FLOWERS TO THE RADIANT DRAUPADI.

A LITTLE LATER, KUBERA'S RAKSHASA GUARDS CAME TO THE LAKE.

IT'S YUDHISH-THIRA !

THE RAKSHASAS BOWED HUMBLY BEFORE HIM.

GO TO YOUR LORD AND TELL HIM THAT I, YUDHISH-THIRA , SEEK HIS PERMISSION TO LIVE FOR A WHILE AT THIS SPOT.

Amar Chitra Katha's

EPICS & MYTHOLOGY

BRAVEHEARTS

VISIONARIES

FABLES & HUMOUR

INDIAN CLASSICS

CONTEMPORARY CLASSICS

EXCITING STORY CATEGORIES,
ONE AMAZING DESTINATION.

From the episodes of Mahabharata to the wit of Birbal,
from the valour of Shivaji to the teachings of Tagore,
from the adventures of Pratapan to the tales of Ruskin Bond –
Amar Chitra Katha stories span across different genres to get you the best of literature.